The Kids Book of
CANADIAN
EXPLORATION

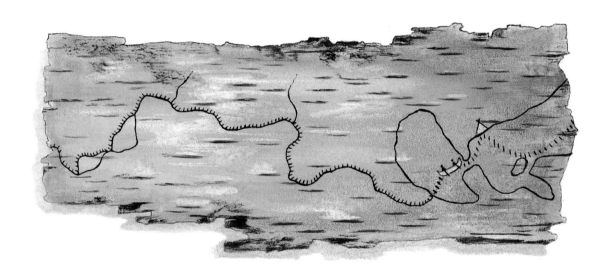

WRITTEN BY

Ann-Maureen Owens & Jane Yealland

ILLUSTRATED BY

John Mantha

KIDS CAN PRESS

To my husband, Peter Owens, for his encouragement, love and support — AMO
To my sister, Joanne Breadner, for all her support and help with research — JY

Acknowledgements

The land that became Canada was explored by men and women from various backgrounds, and this book celebrates the achievements made by many of them. New information about early explorers continues to come to light through research and archaeological work. We are indebted to the superb collections and publications of the Canadian Museum of Civilization and the National Archives of Canada, both located in the nation's capital.

A special thank you to Deanna Brant, Junior Resource Teacher at Quinte Mohawk School, Tyendinaga Mohawk Territory, for her review of the Native exploration pages and to Maurice D. Smith, Curator Emeritus of the Marine Museum of the Great Lakes at Kingston, for his advice and expertise on all things nautical.

Our thanks also to Valerie Hussey for the opportunity to work on this book, Julia Naimska for the creative design elements, and John Mantha for the illustrations that brought the explorers and their adventures to life. As always we are indebted to our wonderful editor, Liz MacLeod, for guiding us through the creation of another book with expertise and grace.

Photo credits

Every reasonable effort has been made to trace ownership of and give accurate credit to copyrighted material. Information that would enable the publisher to correct any discrepancies in future editions would be appreciated.

Abbreviations: t = top; b = bottom; c = centre; l = left; r = right

p. 13: (b) Spanish National Archives, Simancas, Spain; **p. 23:** (r) National Library of Canada; **p. 40:** (l) National Archives of Canada NLC/C-148345, (r) NAC/C-056934; **p. 41:** (t) Courtesy Derek Hayes from *Historical Atlas of Canada: Canada's History Illustrated with Original Maps.*

First paperback edition 2008

Text © 2004 Ann-Maureen Owens and Jane Yealland
Illustrations © 2004 John Mantha

Kids Can Press acknowledges the financial support of the Government of Ontario, through the Ontario Media Development Corporation's Ontario Book Initiative; the Ontario Arts Council; the Canada Council for the Arts; and the Government of Canada, through the BPIDP, for our publishing activity.

Published in Canada by
Kids Can Press Ltd.
29 Birch Avenue
Toronto, ON M4V 1E2

Published in the U.S. by
Kids Can Press Ltd.
2250 Military Road
Tonawanda, NY 14150

www.kidscanpress.com

Edited by Elizabeth MacLeod
Designed by Julia Naimska
Printed and bound in China

The hardcover edition of this book is smyth sewn casebound.
The paperback edition of this book is limp sewn with a drawn-on cover.

CM 04 0 9 8 7 6 5 4 3 2 1
CM PA 08 0 9 8 7 6 5 4 3 2 1

Library and Archives Canada Cataloguing in Publication

Owens, Ann-Maureen
The kids book of Canadian exploration / written by Ann-Maureen Owens & Jane Yealland ; illustrated by John Mantha.

Includes index.
ISBN 978-1-55337-353-7 (bound) ISBN 978-1-55453-257-5 (pbk.)

1. Canada — Discovery and exploration — Juvenile literature.
2. Explorers — Canada — Biography — Juvenile literature.
I. Yealland, Jane II. Mantha, John III. Title.

FC172.O94 2004   j971.01   C2003-906835-8

Kids Can Press is a *forus*™ Entertainment company

CONTENTS

WHAT MAKES AN EXPLORER?

Are you the adventurous type? Would you leave your home, family and friends to sail away over unknown seas to mysterious lands? Hundreds of years ago, that's what explorers who came to Canada did. Like today's astronauts, explorers risked their lives to be the first to discover new places. Back then, it was as scary to sail across the ocean as it is to rocket into outer space today.

The early explorers of Canada had dreams of adventure, fame and fortune. They were brave enough and curious enough to follow their dreams into uncharted waters and new lands. Much of what we know about them comes from the journals, letters and maps they left as evidence of their adventures. Today, you can discover their names in such places as Cabot Strait, Hudson Bay and Vancouver Island.

Sea of Darkness

In the 1400s, many people believed that the world was not round, but so flat that ships could fall off the edge. They thought the Atlantic Ocean — known both as the "Sea of Darkness" and the "Ocean Sea" — was full of ferocious sea monsters.

In those days, people in Europe mostly traded and travelled around the Mediterranean Sea. Its name means "the middle of the world." But they told stories about the places they imagined were across the Atlantic Ocean.

More than 2000 years ago, the Greek philosopher Plato wrote about the amazing wealth of a sunken island called Atlantis. An Irish legend described an island called St. Brendan's Isle as a paradise with a perfect climate and exotic fruits. According to a Portuguese legend, another island known as Antilia had grains of gold in its sand beaches. No wonder people wanted to find these new lands!

Reasons to Explore

Not everyone thought the world was flat. Educated explorers, such as John Cabot, believed that the world was actually round. Cabot was willing to risk the great dangers of exploration to prove that crossing the North Atlantic would be the best trade route to Asia and to be the very first to travel it.

Most explorers were not rich. That meant they needed to convince kings or merchants to provide ships, payment for the crew and enough supplies to last the long journey. To pay back these sponsors, explorers had to claim new lands for their king and country or find new trade routes so the merchants would make more money.

The first Europeans who reached Canada were searching for other places they'd heard about. Instead, they found a completely new land. With the help of the Native people who already lived here, explorers "discovered" a wild and vast country that became Canada.

The Right Stuff

Samuel de Champlain, who founded Quebec in 1608, described the qualities needed to be an explorer: "Above all to be a good man, fearing God ... He had better not be a delicate eater or drinker, otherwise he will be frequently upset by changes of climate and food ... He should be robust and alert, have good sea-legs and be pleasant and affable in conversation ... He must keep a compass below and consult it frequently to see if the ship is on her course."

◆ PROFILE ◆

ST. BRENDAN THE NAVIGATOR

St. Brendan was an Irish monk who explored the stormy North Atlantic Ocean. His small, open, wood-framed boat covered in sewn ox-hides was called a curragh.

According to an Irish legend, St. Brendan and his fellow monks may have even sailed to North America in the sixth century. They probably did get as far as Iceland because the stories of their travels describe "mountains vomiting fire," which sound like Iceland's volcanoes. Also, some places in Iceland have Irish names dating back to St. Brendan's time. Did he go on to reach Canada? No one knows for sure.

Tim Severin and his crew used only oars and a square sail, just as St. Brendan would have used in the sixth century.

History Today

Tim Severin, a modern-day adventurer, proved St. Brendan could have reached Canada. Severin built a replica of St. Brendan's curragh. He and his crew sailed from Ireland in May 1976, wintered in Iceland and arrived in Newfoundland in July 1977. Severin has made it his career to explore the journeys of legendary heroes.

CANADA'S FIRST EXPLORERS

T he exploration of Canada began thousands of years before the arrival of the first European explorer, but it was not written down. Archaeological evidence and oral tradition describe some of the early exploration history of Native people.

Some Native people were key players in the European exploration and settlement of Canada. Native guides took explorers into the interior of the country and shared their knowledge of how to live off the land. Without their help, many explorers would not have survived.

Canada's First Native People

Some anthropologists believe that Canadian Native people are descendants of hunters who migrated here about 40 000 years ago. They came over a land bridge that briefly joined Asia to North America during the ice age. Other scientists think the first explorers of Canada could have arrived even earlier on small boats or rafts from other parts of the world. There is no absolute proof for either of these theories.

Many Native people disagree with the scientific theories of how people came to be in Canada. Each tribe has its own creation story that tells the origins of its people and their relationship with nature.

The six main cultural areas of Canada's First Native People were:

- Arctic
- Subarctic
- Northwest Coast
- Plateau
- Plains
- Eastern Woodlands (hunters)
- Eastern Woodlands (farmers)

First Nations and Inuit

Native people explored all across Canada. Scientists estimate that between 500 000 and 2 million people were living in Canada when the first Europeans arrived. Depending on where they settled, different Native groups developed unique customs and languages. Most tribes belong to one of six groups that still exist today.

The Eastern Woodlands

The Mi'kmaq lived in the Maritime provinces and were the first Native people to trade with Europeans. Huron and Iroquois tribes in Quebec and Ontario farmed beans, corn and squash — "the three sisters." In winter, these large tribes hunted bear, beaver and deer. Huron and Iroquois guides took French and English fur traders to the Great Lakes and beyond.

The Subarctic

The Chipewyan and Cree, wandering hunters of caribou and moose, lived above the treeline in northern Canada. Both tribes traded furs with the

"WE THE ORIGINAL PEOPLES OF THIS LAND KNOW THE CREATOR PUT US HERE. THE CREATOR GAVE US LAWS THAT GOVERN ALL OUR RELATIONSHIPS TO LIVE IN HARMONY WITH NATURE AND MANKIND."

— *A Declaration of the First Nations*

Hudson's Bay Company. They used snowshoes and toboggans to help them travel.

The Plains

In Alberta and Saskatchewan, the Blackfoot, Blood and Peigan were hunters who followed the buffalo. They made pemmican out of dried buffalo meat and later supplied European explorers with this staple food. Before the arrival of the horse, the Plains tribes used dogs to drag their belongings when travelling.

The Plateau

The interior area of British Columbia was home to tribes such as the Interior Salish and the Kootenay. They depended on hunting moose and elk for survival but explored to find and establish trading partnerships with coastal tribes.

The Arctic

The Inuit were a wandering people who hunted seal and walrus. They travelled across the frozen land by dogsled and through icy Arctic waters in sealskin-covered boats. The Inuit had little contact with outsiders until the late 1800s.

The Northwest Coast

The Nootka and the Haida were two of the tribes who lived along the northwest Pacific coast. Because salmon and whales were plentiful, the Haida were able to build permanent villages and explore the coast in their dugout canoes.

Iroquois land is now part of Ontario and Quebec.

Milestone

In the 1500s, the people of the Plains were the first in Canada to ride horses — descendants of ones brought to Mexico by Spanish explorers. On horseback, Native people could hunt more buffalo, escape their enemies and explore farther.

VIKINGS IN CANADA

L eif Ericsson peered through the mist at the rocky shoreline. Was this the new land that his friend Bjarni Herjolfsson had seen fifteen years ago but not investigated? When Ericsson and his men landed on the rocky shore, they found that Native people were already living there. Because the land was covered with trees and vines, Ericsson called it Vinland.

Ericsson and his crew had sailed from Greenland. Originally, the Vikings, also known as the Norse, had come from Northern Europe (Denmark, Norway and Sweden) but had extended their empire to include Iceland and Greenland. Many were farmers, but when they had finished planting their crops, some would become pirates and go "a-viking" — raiding villages along the coasts of Europe

Settlements

At first the Vikings were looking for treasure, but as their population grew, they started looking for land. This was one of the reasons that they risked sailing away from the coastline out into the unknown Atlantic Ocean. Sailing north, the Vikings settled in Iceland. By the year 980, about 30 000 people had immigrated there. A few years later, they began settling what's now Greenland.

Norseman Bjarni Herjolfsson was on his way to Greenland when a fierce storm blew his boat off course. When he finally reached Greenland, he described a new coastline he had seen. Fifteen years later, around 1000, Leif Ericsson bought Herjolfsson's boat and went in search of this new land.

Vinland

Where was the area that Ericsson named Vinland? *The Vinland Sagas* — long poems passed along by word of mouth until they were written down in the 1400s — tell the stories of the Vikings' voyages. Like all good stories, parts were either left out or exaggerated to make them sound more interesting.

The Vinland Sagas tell how Ericsson, his brother Thorvald, his brother-in-law Karlsefni and his sister Freydis all tried to settle in Vinland. It's described as a place with lots of salmon, grapes and enough timber to build their ships, but the sagas don't tell us exactly where it was.

Vinland could have been anywhere on North America's east coast from Newfoundland to the southern coast of New York's Long Island. Historians and scientists still can't agree on its location. The only proven site of a Viking settlement in North America is at L'Anse aux Meadows, discovered in 1960 at the farthest end of northern Newfoundland. If this was Vinland, Ericsson might have lived here, along with about eighty other Norse men and women.

Milestone

The Vinland Sagas tell us that a baby boy was born in Vinland. He was named Snorri, and he may have been the first European child born in Canada.

Skraelings

Who did the Norse meet when they landed in North America? The Vikings called the Native people *skraelings*, an insulting Norse term meaning "scruffy" or "scared." At first the Vikings and Native people traded goods, but they were suspicious of each other, and the sagas tell of battles between the groups.

The Vikings stayed in Canada for only a few years. Why they left is still a mystery. They may have felt threatened by the Native people or maybe, being so far from friends and relatives, they were just homesick.

History Today

L'Anse aux Meadows was first excavated in 1960 by Norwegian archaeologist Anne Stine and her writer husband, Helge Ingstad. They read *The Vinland Sagas* carefully and guessed that the Vikings must have had a settlement somewhere along the Newfoundland coast.

After a long search, aided by a local fisherman who recalled seeing some odd rectangular "humps" in the ground, Stine and Ingstad carefully excavated the site. L'Anse aux Meadows is now a National Historic Site and a UNESCO World Heritage Site that you can visit.

L'Anse aux Meadows

THE HIDDEN CONTINENTS

Most explorers from Europe were unaware of the Vikings' discoveries because their sagas were not widely known. At that time, many European traders were more interested in travelling east to parts of Asia such as China, India and the Philippine Islands. They were looking for silks and spices — luxuries that were in high demand.

In the 1450s, the overland route from Europe to Asia was blocked by a war in the Middle East. Merchants and rulers of Europe were willing to pay explorers to find routes by sea so they could continue this profitable trade. But the Europeans knew very little about how to sail to Asia. Maps from that time show only parts of Africa and Asia. North and South America don't appear at all!

The Columbus Voyages

A young Italian named Christopher Columbus who was working in a map-making shop in Portugal was convinced the world was round. If that was true, he reasoned that sailing west would be a shortcut to Asia.

Portuguese explorers were not interested in Columbus's idea, but King Ferdinand and Queen Isabella of Spain were. In 1492 they sponsored him on this risky venture — a voyage without maps!

Columbus thought he had reached Asia when he landed on the islands now named the West Indies. He called the inhabitants Indians, and their leaders welcomed him with gifts of gold. Ferdinand and Isabella were impressed and sent Columbus back to find more treasure. But his second voyage was not successful in proving he had reached Asia. The new lands that Columbus claimed for Spain did provide gold and silver a few years later, but Columbus died a disappointed man in 1507.

Columbus's First Voyage

ATLANTIC OCEAN

Spain

West Indies

Two Major Powers

Portugal and Spain were the first European nations to explore for riches in what they called the New World. They had the best sailors and the best ships. Other countries were soon jealous of their wealth and possessions. The rulers and merchants of England and France were determined to discover riches for themselves. They also hoped to find a trade route to Asia by exploring the northern part of the New World.

There were two reasons for choosing a northern route. The English and French wanted to stay away from lands to the south held by heavily armed Spaniards. As well, they may have heard rumours of land to the northwest from Icelanders, descendants of the Vikings. Whatever the reason, when explorers from England and France followed a North Atlantic sea route, Canada lay in their path.

Dividing the World

In 1494, the Treaty of Tordesillas gave control over all new lands and sea routes on the west side of an imaginary line in the mid-Atlantic to Spain, and on the east side to

Tall Tales

Centuries before Columbus's voyages, Europeans believed that people living in remote parts of the world were not fully human. Some stories described headless monsters with faces in their chests and people with extra eyes.

Columbus and later explorers were actually surprised that Native people in the New World looked like themselves. To stop Columbus from going too far into their land, the Native people of the West Indies warned him off with stories of wild people with tails who lived in the forest.

Portugal. Since it was hard to make accurate measurements at sea, no one knew exactly where the boundary lay.

Most of Canada would have been in the Spanish half of the world, but the Portuguese thought Labrador and Newfoundland were on their side of the line. England and France were angry about being left out of the treaty but could not risk going to war with Spain or Portugal, the most powerful countries at that time.

Map-makers used information from explorers to draw maps.

The New World was called America after the Italian sailor Amerigo Vespucci, who made at least two voyages there and wrote popular books about his travels. In 1507, a German map-maker who must have read these books put Amerigo's name on the continent, and others copied his map.

JOHN CABOT

John Cabot had a dream. Ever since he'd sailed the Mediterranean Sea as a boy, he'd wanted to be the captain of his own ship and voyage across the mysterious Atlantic Ocean.

Cabot was born Giovanni Caboto in 1451 in Genoa, Italy, the same year and place as Christopher Columbus. Like Columbus, Caboto believed that sailing west was the easiest way to the East. But he calculated that the shortest route would be a northern one. When Caboto moved to Bristol, England, with his wife and three sons to find sponsors for his voyage, he became known as John Cabot.

Exploring for England

English merchants who had heard the news about Columbus's discoveries were eager to find a route across the Atlantic Ocean, too. Cabot was chosen for this exploration because King Henry VII liked his proposed route across the North Atlantic best. It was far enough from where Columbus had landed to not cause a war with Spain.

Cabot's dream of crossing the Atlantic became a reality when he was made captain of a small ship called the *Matthew*. His job was to discover any "new" lands, whether or not people were already living there.

Cabot's First Voyage

Cabot set sail in late May of 1497 and, after five weeks at sea, dropped anchor at a rocky, empty shore. He found some signs of life, such as traps set to catch animals and the ashes of a cooking fire, but met no

The *Matthew* set sail with a crew of nineteen men.

people. He decided this was "New Found Land" and claimed it for England by putting up a cross.

Cabot travelled south along what's now known as the east coast of North America and was impressed by the great number of codfish. Until the end of the twentieth century, the shallow water that extends far off the coastline, called the Grand Banks, was one of the best fishing grounds in the world.

DID YOU KNOW

European rulers did not recognize the rights of Native people and felt they could claim any land and seize all property. Today Native groups are still trying to reclaim their ancestors' land and their rights to hunt and fish.

Fishermen came from Europe to fish the Grand Banks, off Newfoundland.

Cabot's Second Voyage

When Cabot returned to England in August, the Bristol merchants were disappointed that he didn't bring silks, spices and gold. However, King Henry VII was delighted because he thought England now owned part of Asia. Cabot was pleased to receive a reward of £10 (worth $15 000 in today's money) and a pension of £20 a year. The king also provided Cabot with the money for a second voyage with five ships to the New Found Land in 1498.

"THE SEA IN THESE PARTS HOLDS GREAT QUANTITIES OF FISH, WHICH MAY BE TAKEN BY MERELY LOWERING A WEIGHTED BASKET INTO THE WATER."

— *John Cabot*

Rumours and Lies

Most historians say Cabot and his crew were lost in storms at sea while exploring the east coast of Canada. According to another rumour, he returned to England but was quickly forgotten because he failed to bring back riches. One of Cabot's sons, Sebastian, caused even more confusion by claiming his father's discoveries for himself, but historians uncovered the lie.

In any case, New Found Land had no gold or spices to offer. England lost interest in exploring North America for a few hundred years, until the trade in fish and furs became more valuable.

Trade Secrets

English fishermen may have discovered the Grand Banks years before Cabot, but they kept it a

trade secret. An undated letter (below) written in Spanish from a Bristol merchant named John Day and addressed to Columbus hints at this secret. Day had trading partners in Spain and may have benefited if Columbus knew about Cabot's discovery of an island in the western Atlantic Ocean.

Day's letter, found in 1955, went on to give further information about English voyages to the west. It also hints that Bristol fishermen may have found this same land "in times past."

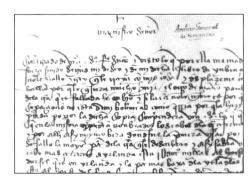

TECHNOLOGY OF EXPLORATION I:
NAVIGATIONAL TOOLS

Explorers who dared go beyond familiar landmarks into open sea had to be skilled navigators. After all, when you can see only water everywhere, how do you find your way?

Just like modern navigators who study satellite transmissions to calculate their position at sea, early explorers looked to the sky for guidance. They used astronomers' tools to find the position of the sun and the stars. Explorers' observations of weather, wind and water also helped them find their way.

Compasses

A thousand years ago, Chinese navigators began suspending a sliver of magnetic iron ore over a slab marked with the directions north, south, east and west. Europeans learned about this tool called the compass and began using it about 200 years later. The compass still allows sailors to find their direction in any weather, day or night, because its needle always points north.

Quadrants

One of the first tools used to measure latitude in the 1400s was this quarter circle with degrees marked on it like a protractor. Sailors lined up the quadrant's sights with the North Star and read the ship's latitude by where the string hung along the arc.

Cross-staffs

Because it could be cheaply made from wood, the cross-staff came into wide use by sailors in the mid-1400s. Latitude was measured by sliding the crosspiece until one end lined up with the horizon and the other with the North Star.

Latitude: How Far North or South?

Sailors use lines of latitude drawn on a map to calculate how far north or south they are from the equator, an imaginary line around the middle of Earth halfway between the North and South Poles. The angle between the horizon and the North Star, which has a fixed position above the North Pole, changes depending on the ship's latitude. This is also true for the position of the noon sun. To calculate their ship's location using these angle measurements, explorers had to be good mathematicians.

Astrolabes

First used by Arabs around 1300 to find their way across the desert, the astrolabe was later adopted by European countries for ocean navigation. Because it was suspended by a thumb ring, gravity did the work of aligning the astrolabe. This meant that it was not necessary to see the horizon. The metal pointer could be lined up with the North Star even on the darkest nights — but only on a calm sea.

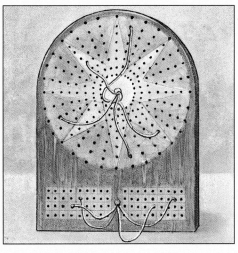

Traverse Boards

Until the 1700s, explorers used the traverse board, a circular piece of wood marked with holes along each compass point, to keep track of their course. Every thirty minutes a peg had to be put in one of the holes. The cabin boy kept track of time by turning over the half-hour hourglass.

Chronometers

In 1761, British clockmaker John Harrison invented the chronometer. He had worked for fifty years to perfect this timepiece that didn't need a pendulum. The chronometer could be used to measure longitude at sea.

Sextants

In the mid-eighteenth century, the British developed the sextant, an improvement on the quadrant. It was an arrangement of mirrors with a movable index arm that could pinpoint the ship's latitude very accurately. Just as a stopwatch measures speed to 0.01 of a second, the sextant measures latitude to 0.01 of a degree.

Longitude: How Far East or West?

The problem of how to measure lines of longitude on a map was difficult to solve. For centuries, sailors estimated the distance they travelled by "dead reckoning." This involved finding the ship's speed by throwing pieces of wood overboard and using an hourglass to see how long it took the ship to pass them. Navigators then used the speed to calculate how far they had sailed from home.

But measuring speed and time was tough. Early clocks depended on the steady swing of a pendulum, and so they were useless on the pitching, rolling deck of a sailing ship.

THE PORTUGUESE IN CANADA

Beginning in the 1440s, Portuguese sailors ventured farther and farther out into the Atlantic Ocean. They were expert navigators who discovered and settled islands in the middle of the Atlantic — midway between Portugal and Canada — called the Azores. There are few written records of these voyages because many of these explorers were lost at sea.

Portugal's main focus in the 1500s was exploring trade routes along the African coast to India, but explorers from the Azores were interested in sailing farther west. Along with Basque whalers, who came from the northern provinces of Spain, and fishermen from England and France, the Portuguese developed the fishing industry on Canada's east coast.

Missing Brothers

The next year, the Corte-Real brothers sailed three ships to Newfoundland. The ship that Gaspar captained never returned, but the other two came back with human cargo — fifty-seven men and one woman who had been captured to be slaves. Historians believe these captives were probably Beothuks, Newfoundland's Native people. Miguel went back to look for Gaspar, and Miguel, too, was lost at sea.

Labrador

Joao Fernandes, a sailor from the Azores, was known by his title, *lavrador*, which means "small landowner." He traded with the merchants of Bristol, England, and it's likely that Fernandes sailed to Newfoundland with John Cabot. Around 1500, Fernandes reached Greenland and called it *Tiera del lavrador* (Land of the Landowner). Later the name was used for the part of Canada called Labrador.

Sturdy ships, called caravels, were designed by the Portuguese to explore the Atlantic Ocean.

The Corte-Reals

Gaspar Corte-Real and his brother Miguel (right) were also from the Azores. Gaspar sailed for King Manuel I of Portugal, who gave him permission to explore and claim new lands in the North Atlantic. In 1500 he sailed towards Greenland and then on to Newfoundland.

Whalers went out in small boats, called dories, to harpoon the right whales.

Fish Discovery

Portuguese explorers soon realized that Newfoundland, although not part of Asia, still had treasure — fish. The coastal waters were full of cod, large fish with firm white flesh that are easy to catch. Fish was in big demand in Europe since most of the people were Christians and church rules did not allow them to eat meat for 160 days a year. Fish was a popular substitute for meat on those days.

The Portuguese and Basques found that when covered in salt, cod could be preserved for the long trip home across the Atlantic. Portuguese fishermen rushed to take advantage of this rich resource.

Cape Breton Colony

In 1520, Joao Alvarez Fagundes explored the south coast of Newfoundland. Historians believe he may have started a colony on the coast of Cape Breton Island.

The Whalers

For at least 100 years, whalers from France and Spain made yearly voyages to the Strait of Belle Isle between Labrador and Newfoundland. They hunted baleen and right whales for their oil, which was used as heating fuel in Europe. During the 1500s, thousands of whales were killed.

The Right Whale

Hunting whales has always been a dangerous activity. The Inuit hunted from kayaks, while the Europeans used small open boats. Once the whale was struck with a harpoon, the hunters had to hang on until the whale became exhausted.

The hunters' favourite whale was a large, slow swimmer. Best of all, when it was killed it would float. Because of these qualities, it was nicknamed the "right" whale and hunted almost to extinction. Today, the right whale is a protected species.

History Today

The world's largest whaling port in the sixteenth century is now a National Historic Site at Red Bay, Labrador. Visitors can see a reconstructed whaling station and a 500-year-old whaling ship.

JACQUES CARTIER

When John Cabot's report of the huge fish stocks in Newfoundland reached France, many fishermen were quick to explore the Grand Banks, including a young boy named Jacques Cartier, who went there on many fishing trips with his father. He wondered what lay beyond the distant coast of Newfoundland. Eventually, as captain of his own ship, Cartier explored the land that so fascinated him.

Compared with England, Portugal and Spain, France was late in sending explorers to the New World. But the French king finally decided he didn't want to be left out when it came to searching for a route to Asia or for riches in the New World.

Verranzzano's Voyage

In 1523, the French King François I sent Giovanni da Verranzzano, an Italian sailor, to explore the coastline from modern-day Florida to Newfoundland for a passage to Asia. Verranzzano mapped 3220 km (2000 mi.) of this previously unknown coastline and proved that North America was a continent, not a cluster of islands as many people thought. But he failed to find a route to Asia.

In his ship's log, Verranzzano (above) described friendly Native people who offered him a peace pipe to smoke, which seemed strange to him because he had never seen tobacco. Sadly, Verranzzano repaid this hospitality by kidnapping a Native boy to take back and show off to the king.

Fishermen's Tales

It was ten years before the French king sponsored another voyage of exploration to North America, and he chose Jacques Cartier to lead this expedition. King François I had heard French fishermen's stories of a large body of water beyond Newfoundland and thought Cartier, a former fisherman who had been to Newfoundland, could find it. Could this be the way to a passage to Asia?

When Cartier reached Newfoundland, he saw animals he'd never seen before.

Cartier's First Voyage

Cartier set off for Newfoundland in 1534, and when he reached it, he sailed around its northern tip. In these unknown waters, the sailors were on the lookout for sea monsters. Instead, they saw animals that were new to them: gannets, great auks (now extinct), polar bears and walrus.

When Cartier came to a channel stretching westward, he hoped this would be the passage to Asia. It turned out to be the waterway that separates Labrador and Newfoundland, now called the Strait of Belle Isle.

Milestone

Cartier's trade with members of the Mi'kmaq tribe was the first recorded trade between Native people and Europeans.

Meeting the Mi'kmaqs

Cartier entered what he called a "Great Bay" — the Gulf of St. Lawrence, the mouth of the river — and landed on the coasts of Prince Edward Island, New Brunswick and the Gaspé peninsula of Quebec. At a place he named Chaleur Bay, which means "bay of heat" (it was a hot summer day), Cartier and his men were surrounded by about fifty Native people in birchbark canoes. He nervously fired two shots that made them retreat, but the next day the Mi'kmaqs came back (above), waving animal skins that they traded for axes, beads and knives.

Meeting the Iroquois

Some days later in Gaspé Bay, the French were greeted by more than 200 members of a different tribe, the Iroquois. They were on a fishing trip from their home, Stadacona, the site of present-day Quebec City. The two groups enjoyed a feast together, but the mood changed when Cartier's men put up a 9 m (30 ft.) cross inscribed "Long Live the King of France."

The Iroquois chief, Donnacona, realized that the French were claiming land that rightly belonged to his people, so he paddled out to the ships with his sons to protest. Cartier managed to get the chief's two sons, Domagaya and Taignoagny, aboard his ship and gave them fine clothes. He indicated to Donnacona that he wanted to take them back to France to meet the king but would return with them the next spring. Donnacona had no choice but to let them go.

"THE FINEST LAND ONE CAN SEE AND FULL OF BEAUTIFUL TREES AND MEADOWS."

— *Jacques Cartier, describing Prince Edward Island*

Cartier meeting the Iroquois of Hochelaga.

Hochelaga

The Kingdom of the Saguenay

Domagaya and Taignoagny, Donnacona's kidnapped sons, were taught French so they could be guides and interpreters for Cartier. They told King François I that a rich land full of gold, silver and copper called "The Kingdom of the Saguenay" existed beyond the "River of Canada." That was all the French king needed to hear. He sent Cartier back to stay for more than a year and return with treasure.

Cartier's Second Voyage

In 1535, Domagaya and Taignoagny showed Cartier the way to the River of Canada, and Cartier renamed it the St. Lawrence River. When they arrived at Stadacona, Donnacona tried to scare the French from going any farther up the river because he wanted to control trade with the French. But Cartier and thirty-five of his men continued to Hochelaga, the site of present-day Montreal.

Hochelaga was an impressive palisaded village of 2000 Iroquois, but Cartier was disappointed to find only cornfields, fur clothing and shell ornaments instead of the gold, silver, silks and spices he was looking for. By climbing a nearby mountain, today called Mount Royal, he could see the rapids that would stop his ship from going any farther.

Trust and Betrayal

By late winter, most of the French in Stadacona were suffering from a disease called scurvy and twenty-five of them had died. Domagaya saved the rest by sharing the Native cure for this disease — a tea of white cedar needles called *annedda*. When spring came, Cartier decided to return to France.

Before leaving, Cartier kidnapped ten Iroquois, including Chief Donnacona. He regarded them as trophies to show the king, and he hoped Donnacona's stories of wealth in the Kingdom of Saguenay would encourage the king to finance another exploration. Cartier promised to bring them back home but the Iroquois all died in France.

Cartier's Third Voyage

The third voyage in 1541 was not just for exploration but also to establish a French colony in the New World. If there were riches in North America, such as the Spanish were finding in South America, France wanted a colony there to protect her claim and to be a base for further exploration. A nobleman, the Sieur

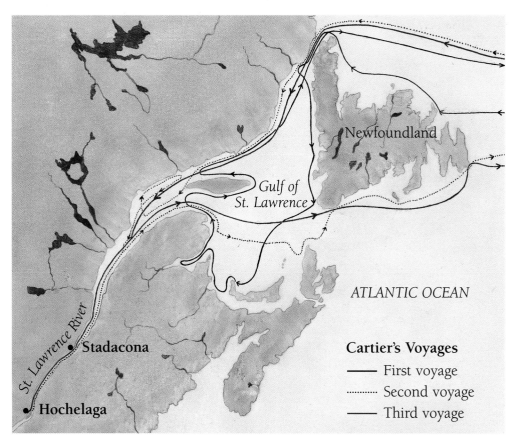

Newfoundland

Gulf of St. Lawrence

ATLANTIC OCEAN

St. Lawrence River

● **Stadacona**

● **Hochelaga**

Cartier's Voyages
—— First voyage
·········· Second voyage
—— Third voyage

de Roberval, was to be the governor in charge, but Cartier's job was to explore for the riches that his captive, Donnacona, had claimed were there.

Canadian Diamonds

The new colony was established near Stadacona. Cartier discovered shiny rocks there that he thought were precious stones. To mine the large amount that he wanted to take home, he had to endure a cold winter fighting off the now hostile Iroquois. That spring Cartier sailed away with a ship full of "gold and diamonds." But his cargo turned out to be nothing more than fool's gold and quartz.

Since most of Roberval's colonists were not prepared for harsh winters and Iroquois attacks, they returned to France a year later and Roberval announced the colony was a failure. However, he had cruelly left some colonists behind.

◆ **PROFILE** ◆

MARGUERITE DE LA ROCHE

As the colonists made their way to Stadacona in the summer of 1542, Roberval was outraged to discover a secret love affair between his unmarried niece, Marguerite de la Roche, and one of his young sailors. Roberval cast de la Roche off the ship with her elderly maid onto a rocky island known as the Isle of Demons on the north shore of the Gulf of St. Lawrence. Her sweetheart jumped ship to be with her, and eventually they had a baby.

Because of the eerie sounds made by the wind blowing around the island's sheer cliffs, fishermen were usually too superstitious to go near it. Finally, after more than two years, a ship's captain noticed smoke from a signal fire. By then de la Roche was the only survivor.

DID YOU KNOW

The Iroquois suspected the French of giving them a mysterious illness, which was probably smallpox.

THE NORTHWEST PASSAGE

In spite of finding fish, furs and timber in Canada, explorers still saw the land as just an obstacle in the way of getting to the East. The English were interested in finding a passage through Canada — what they called a Northwest Passage to Asia. It would be far away from the Spanish and Portuguese, who had control of the routes to the south.

No one knew for sure if there even was a Northwest Passage, but many believed that the northern part of North America was made up of islands and that there must be a way through them. The search for a Northwest Passage took hundreds of years and cost thousands of lives. Many explorers became lost in the ice and froze, starved to death or were shipwrecked by icebergs.

The Pirate Explorer

Martin Frobisher was always looking for ways to make money — he was even a pirate for a few years. But after reading Gilbert's book about the Northwest Passage, Frobisher (below) became determined to be an explorer and find a route through North America to Asia.

Gilbert's Theory

Humphrey Gilbert was an English soldier and navigator who believed a Northwest Passage must exist. In 1576 he wrote a book, *A Discourse of a Discoverie for a New Passage to Cataia* (China).

Gilbert never tested his theory, but he did reach Newfoundland in 1583 (above). When he sailed into the harbour of what is now St. John's, he found thirty-four fishing boats from many European countries. Gilbert claimed the land for Queen Elizabeth I with such authority that when he demanded all the other ships' captains pay him a tax, they did.

Only one of his three ships, the *Golden Hind*, returned to England, but Gilbert was not on board. He had stubbornly insisted on staying on his smallest vessel, the *Squirrel*, and it was swallowed up by the ocean waves.

In 1576, Frobisher sailed west of Greenland and discovered a waterway that he felt was the Northwest Passage. He named it Frobisher Strait. Believing he had reached Asia, Frobisher brought back to England rocks containing bits of metal that he thought were "Asian gold."

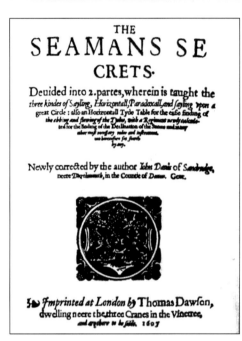

DID YOU KNOW

Like Martin Frobisher, many people have been fooled by rocks that glitter. This shimmering is caused by flecks of mica, a mineral that was used for making early mirrors. The fool's gold Frobisher brought back to England was used to pave the streets of London.

Back for More

Frobisher immediately returned to Canada, but this time he didn't bother looking for a passage. He was searching for more gold. He brought with him 150 miners (above) and returned with 200 t (220 tn.) of his precious rocks.

To prove he'd discovered Asia, Frobisher captured a man, a woman and a child on Baffin Island and took them back to England. Within a month, all three died. They were probably Inuit, but the English believed they were Asians.

Final Voyage

Frobisher came back to Canada again in 1578, now with 15 ships, 300 miners and the supplies needed to start a colony. Due to bad weather, he lost so many ships and men he couldn't start a colony, but it didn't stop him from mining.

When Frobisher returned to England with more rocks, he discovered that tests done on the metal while he was away proved it was worthless fool's gold. He quickly left the country and returned to being a pirate.

Author and Inventor

Sponsored by merchants from London, England, John Davis made three voyages from 1585 to 1587 in search of a Northwest Passage. Davis mapped much of the Arctic coast and wrote about the weather and the Inuit. His book, *The Seaman's Secrets* (above) was a favourite of sailors. Davis was also known as the inventor of the back-staff, a navigation instrument (it was an improvement on the cross-staff — see page 14).

However, Davis's search for the Northwest Passage was unsuccessful. He spent the rest of his life exploring the south Pacific Ocean, where he was murdered by Japanese pirates in 1605.

One of Frobisher's ships crushed by ice.

TECHNOLOGY OF EXPLORATION II:
SHIPBUILDING

As explorers sailed farther from home, shipbuilding had to change. Crossing the ocean required larger and stronger ships than had been needed to sail along the European coast. Ship construction, sail design and especially the invention of the rudder were the major shipbuilding developments that helped explorers.

Rudders

For centuries, sailors used oars on both sides of the ship to steer a course. The Vikings were the first to use a single steering oar or "steerboard" hung over the right side. That is why that side of the ship later became known as the starboard side. By about 1250, this oar gradually developed into a fixed rudder at the stern. A rudder, moving from side to side on an axle, could steer the ship more effectively.

Sail Design

From the twelfth to the fourteenth centuries, ships in the north of Europe used a large square sail that could be shortened in bad weather and swivelled to catch the wind. The triangular sails of Southern European ships were more efficient for manoeuvring around coastlines.

As ships became larger, more masts were added with both types of sails — square ones to sail the oceans and triangular ones to navigate the rivers.

Ship Construction

The Viking ships were "clinker-built" — the boards of the hull overlapped. Today this method of constructing the shell of a vessel is used only for small boats.

By the 1400s, European explorers and merchants wanted bigger and faster ships to cross the ocean, so the "carvel-built" style became popular. In these ships the hull planks were butted edge to edge and bolted to a frame of keel, stem, stern and ribs.

Clinker-built

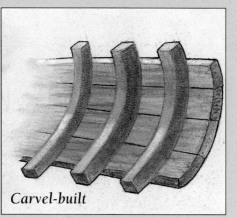

Carvel-built

Caravels

Early in the fifteenth century, Prince Henry the Navigator of Portugal invented the caravel to weather the fierce Atlantic storms. It was carvel-built, with a square stern and fixed rudder, high decks or "castles" at each end, three masts and a mixture of square and triangular sails.

The ships that brought explorers to Canada, such as Cabot's *Matthew*, were caravels. They were considered small even back then — about the size of a large houseboat today. Their size made them easy to manoeuvre.

Ship Size

By the 1500s, ships were measured by the amount of cargo they could carry. A typical caravel could carry from 40 to 80 barrels of wine or beer called *tons,* from the Spanish word for "barrel," *tonel*. On ships a ton is a measurement of volume equal to 1.1 m³ (40 cu. ft.), not a measurement of weight.

DID YOU KNOW

Since a ship's hold was crowded with cargo, sailors had no place to sleep. So when Christopher Columbus described how Native people of the West Indies used hammocks, these were quickly adopted by European sailors. Hammocks could easily be put up at night and removed in the morning — plus they were comfortable!

Caravel

Carracks

For voyages of more than three months, explorers used the larger carrack, which could carry all the provisions needed for longer voyages. Jacques Cartier's carrack, the *Grande Hermine*, held 150 to 180 m³ (3640 to 4365 cu. ft.) of provisions, enough to last through the Canadian winter.

Galleons

In the sixteenth and seventeenth centuries, the galleon, larger and faster than the caravel or carrack, was used by most European fleets. It had four masts and could transport six times as much cargo as a carrack. Armed with a cannon, galleons were also used as warships. Francis Drake sailed his galleon the *Golden Hind* around the world in 1577 and explored some of Canada's west coast.

Merchant men

Merchantmen were trading ships, the supertankers of their time. In the eighteenth century, James Cook's *Endeavour* was large enough to carry all the equipment needed by the scientists who accompanied him.

Galleon

SAMUEL DE CHAMPLAIN

The French king François I gave up on a settlement in the New World after Jacques Cartier's failure to find riches there in 1542. But French fishermen continued to visit Canada's east coast and began trading metal tools and woven blankets for bear and beaver skins from the Native people. Animal furs became luxuries in Europe, and gaining control of Canada, the source of these furs, became a new way to make money. France's interest in claiming land in the New World was rekindled.

One exceptional person, Samuel de Champlain, was mainly responsible for establishing France's colony in Canada. Champlain was exceptional because he was not only a soldier and a ship's captain, but also an explorer, a geographer, a map-maker, a trader and a writer. He was so dedicated to the colony of Quebec that he was called the "Father of New France."

Introducing Religion

Because he was a very religious man, Champlain thought it was necessary to convert Native people to Christianity. In France, this idea became so popular that many religious people went to Quebec to help (see page 30). In 1642, Montreal was founded as the missionary colony Ville-Marie.

"BY TAKING THE HELP OF THE INDIANS AND THEIR CANOES, A MAN MAY SEE ALL THAT IS TO BE SEEN WITHIN THE SPACE OF A YEAR OR TWO."

— *Champlain, in his book* Des Sauvages

New France

Champlain (above) was not a nobleman, a huge disadvantage to getting ahead in those days, but the son of a common seaman. Champlain first came to Canada in 1603 as a French soldier on a fur-trading expedition up the St. Lawrence River.

In 1605, Champlain helped set up a fur-trading colony at Port-Royal, on the north shore of Nova Scotia. He made detailed maps of what are now the coasts of Nova Scotia, New Brunswick and New England. But Champlain was convinced that inland along the St. Lawrence River was a better fur-trading area, so in 1608 he built "the Habitation," a colony at Quebec. It became the centre of New France.

"The Habitation," Quebec

Friends and Enemies

Champlain was eager to explore west of Quebec and establish a fur-trading alliance with the Huron who lived there. That's why in 1609 he agreed to join a war party (above) against their enemies, the Iroquois. On the lake that would later be named for Champlain in today's New York State, Champlain shot three Iroquois chiefs with his musket, a weapon the Iroquois had never seen before. From then on, the Iroquois were the enemy of the French.

Lost and Found

With the Huron, Champlain travelled for two years by canoe as far west as Lake Huron, returning to Quebec in 1616. While portaging near Green Lake, Ontario, Champlain dropped his astrolabe (see page 15). A young farm boy found it in 1867, and it's now in the Canadian Museum of Civilization in Hull, Quebec.

Madame Champlain

On a trip back to France in 1610, Champlain married a twelve-year-old girl, Hélène Boullé. She brought to the marriage a lot of money, which Champlain needed to support his travels and his struggling colony. Hélène remained with her parents until she was older. Champlain finally brought his wife to Quebec ten years later, but she stayed only four years — she much preferred life in Paris.

◆ PROFILE ◆

MATHIEU DA COSTA

Mathieu Da Costa is known as the first Black explorer of Canada. It's thought he came to Canada on a Portuguese fishing vessel and learned to speak the Mi'kmaq language. In 1604, he acted as the interpreter at Port-Royal. Da Costa helped bring about friendly relations between the French and the Mi'kmaq.

DID YOU KNOW

Samuel de Champlain died at Quebec City in 1635 and was buried beneath Notre Dame Church. It's said that his bones still lie there, but they have never been positively identified.

HENRY HUDSON

At the same time as Champlain was exploring the Quebec area, Henry Hudson, an English explorer, was searching North America for a passage to Asia. In the years from 1607 to 1611, he sailed for both Holland and England.

Hudson had the determination and navigation skills to be a good explorer, but he wasn't a strong leader. He was a poor judge of character, and some of the men he chose for his crew were troublemakers. Hudson was also hard to get along with and was so obsessed with finding a route to Asia that he ignored the needs of his men.

Hudson's Explorations

Henry Hudson (above) made four voyages in four years searching for a route to Asia. The first two voyages, financed by English merchants, were to find a northeast passage around the top of Europe and Russia to China and Japan. Hudson's attempts were blocked by ice and heavy winds in both 1607 and 1608. But his reputation as a determined explorer spread to Holland.

Sailing for the Dutch

Exploring for a group of merchants called the Dutch East India Company on his third voyage in 1609, Hudson changed course and crossed the Atlantic Ocean to North America to look for a Northwest Passage. He found the bay now called New York Harbor and sailed up the river that is today named after him. But the farther north Hudson went, the more

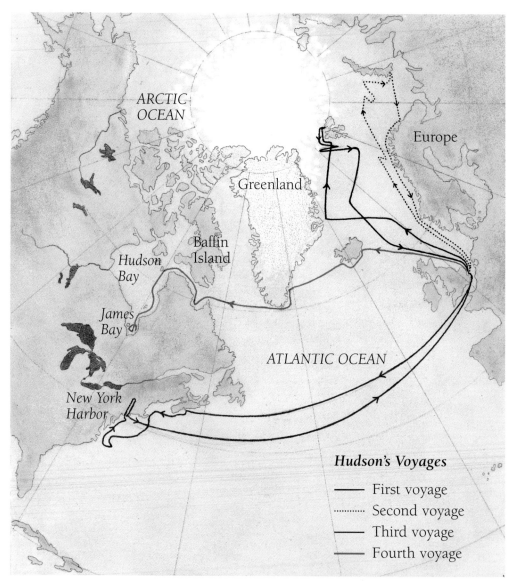

Hudson's Voyages
— First voyage
·········· Second voyage
— Third voyage
— Fourth voyage

he realized this was not the way to the Pacific Ocean and Asia, so he returned to Europe.

Sailing for England Again

In 1610, Hudson headed his ship the *Discovery* for the Arctic Ocean north of Canada. He and his crew navigated through treacherous tides and ice

south of Baffin Island to a large body of salt water. This, Hudson thought, must be the Pacific Ocean, but he had really discovered Hudson Bay. After several weeks of exploring into what's now known as James Bay, he came to a dead end. By then winter was setting in, and it was too late to sail back home.

Mutiny

Things went from bad to worse. Because he was moody and stern, Hudson was not a popular leader, and now he couldn't even bribe the men with a bonus to keep looking for the Northwest Passage. Trapped in the ice without enough food, the crew suspected Hudson and his favourites of taking more than their share.

When spring finally came, the crew was afraid their captain would continue searching for the Northwest Passage, so they set Hudson, his son and six supporters adrift in an open boat called a shallop (above). They were never seen again.

"NOW WERE ALL THE POOR MEN PUT IN THE SHALLOP ... AND [THE MUTINEERS] CUT HER BOW ROPE FROM THE STERN OF OUR SHIP. WE SAW NOT THE SHALLOP EVER AFTER."

— *Abucok Prickett, survivor of Hudson's last voyage*

Pardon

The punishment for taking over a ship and putting the captain overboard was death by hanging. However, when the mutineers on Hudson's ship sailed the *Discovery* back to England, they were allowed to live. Since they had new knowledge of Canada's Arctic Ocean, they were too valuable to be hanged.

Exploring the Big Bay

Many explorers followed Hudson's route, including Thomas Button, who sailed the *Discovery* back to look for Hudson, unsuccessfully, the following year. In 1631, two English explorers met in Hudson Bay by chance. These rivals were both searching for the Northwest Passage, but neither Thomas James (for whom James Bay is named) nor Luke "North-West" Fox found it. Fox's map of northern Canada, mistakenly showing no possible Northwest Passage, stopped the search for a passage for more than a century.

History Today

Hudson Bay and James Bay are still isolated areas but can now be visited by train. Passengers take the "Polar Bear Express" from Cochrane, Ontario, to Moosonee on the shores of James Bay, or the "Hudson Bay" from Winnipeg to Churchill, Manitoba.

MISSIONARY EXPLORERS

In the early 1600s, explorers were searching for routes to Asia or riches in the New World, but the French priests who came with them were searching for souls. These young men were so committed to their beliefs that they were willing to suffer hardships, starvation and even death for their cause.

The priests travelled far into Canada's wilderness, but they would not have survived without the help of the people they came to save. From the Native people, the missionaries learned how to paddle, snowshoe and find food in the forests. The priests kept records of their travels and drew maps of their explorations, which were helpful to other explorers who followed.

Native Religions

All Native people had their own religion. The priests could not see that many of the rituals that Native people practised were similar to their own. For example, before canoeing over dangerous rapids, the Huron would ask their God for help by sprinkling the river with special herbs. The priests would seek God's protection for their mission forts by sprinkling them with holy water.

The Récollets

The first priests to come to Canada were invited by Samuel de Champlain in 1615. The Récollets made visits to Huron villages but did not have the financial support to set up any permanent missions.

The Jesuits

A larger and more well-off order, the Jesuits arrived in New France in 1625 to take the Récollets' place. Joining the Jesuits was like joining the army. Training to become a Jesuit priest was rigorous and took up to fifteen years.

Travelling throughout Huron country, the Jesuits preached about Christianity to the Native people. Often they were the first Europeans to reach remote areas, and their careful records helped map-makers produce more accurate maps of New France.

Jesuit priest exploring with Huron natives.

Missions

The Jesuits set up missions near Native villages to offer medical help and religious education. The largest mission was Sainte-Marie Among the Hurons. The priests, called Black Robes by the Hurons because of their clothing, unknowingly brought germs with them. Native people had no natural protection against European diseases, and thousands of them died.

By 1639 these diseases, particularly smallpox, had reduced the Huron nation from 25 000 people to 9000. Many of the Huron blamed the Jesuits for their suffering.

The Priest-Explorer

Father Jacques Marquette was a Jesuit priest who, in 1673, joined the French-Canadian explorer Louis Jolliet in his search for a passage to the Pacific Ocean. Along the way, Father Marquette hoped to baptize Native people.

The two men, together with three Native guides, paddled more than 2500 km (1550 mi.) down the Mississippi River but were disappointed to discover that it flowed into the Gulf of Mexico, not the Pacific Ocean. Marquette never regained his strength after this difficult trip, and at age thirty-eight died of typhoid, a deadly fever.

FATHER JEAN DE BRÉBEUF

Jesuit Father Jean de Brébeuf spent twenty-four years as a missionary in Canada. An expert in the Huron language and culture, he built a mission fort near Georgian Bay called Sainte-Marie Among the Hurons. Father Brébeuf even wrote "The Huron Christmas Carol," which is still sung today.

In 1649, Iroquois warriors battling the Huron over control of the fur trade captured Father Brébeuf, another priest and their Huron converts. They were all tortured to death.

History Today

The Jesuits built Sainte-Marie Among the Hurons as a fortified mission. After only ten years the Jesuits burned the mission to the ground in 1649 rather than surrendering it to the attacking Iroquois. You can visit a replica of the mission in Midland, Ontario.

The *Relations*

The Jesuit *Relations* were annual reports sent back to France that described in great detail the missionaries' travels and work among the Native people. In Europe they were very popular as travel literature. The Relations remain one of the most complete written records of life in early Canada.

Jesuit priest preaching at Sainte-Marie Among the Hurons.

TECHNOLOGY OF EXPLORATION III:
WILDERNESS SURVIVAL

Would you eat your shoes if you were starving? That's what Arctic explorers had to do when they ran out of food. Surviving food shortages, harsh winters and hordes of mosquitoes took skill and stamina.

Europeans who copied the Native ways of dealing with the dangers and problems of exploration had a better chance of making it in Canada. The explorers who continued to believe that they were superior and that Native people could not teach them anything often paid the ultimate price — losing their lives.

Birchbark Canoes

When Samuel de Champlain arrived in Canada in 1603, he soon realized that the only way to explore its rivers and streams was by using Huron birchbark canoes. These light canoes could be paddled and portaged over shallow waters where bigger boats couldn't go.

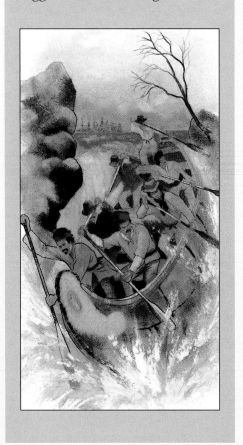

Snowshoes

Snowshoes were used by almost every Native group in Canada. To keep from sinking in deep snow, the Native people used the clever idea of spreading a person's weight over an area larger than his or her foot. They based the shape of the snowshoe on animal tracks such as those made by bears, beavers and foxes.

The size of the snowshoes depended on how deep the snow was and whether the Native people were hunting or carrying heavy packs. Ash or pine boughs were used for the frame and were held together by woven strips of rawhide. European explorers quickly realized showshoes were an ideal way to get through heavy snow.

Toboggans

Toboggans, like snowshoes, were useful for moving people and supplies over snow. They were made from two pieces of birch lashed together with thongs of deerskin. If there was no wood, a frozen animal skin was used instead, and sometimes even a large piece of frozen meat.

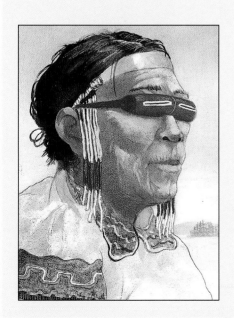

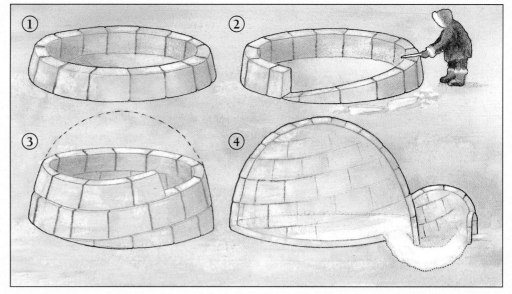

Snowhouses

One danger of exploring in the Arctic was being caught in a sudden blizzard. The solution was to carve out blocks of snow and build a snow house, called an igloo by the Inuit. A skilled explorer could build one (above) in twenty to thirty minutes. The heat created by people inside the igloo would melt the inside walls, which would then freeze into ice, making the snow house very strong.

Caches

Sometimes explorers were travelling for months. They couldn't carry enough food for the return trip, so they copied the Native idea of storing food and supplies under large piles of rocks. These caches also served as landmarks. Robert Peary (see page 48) left several caches on his trek to the North Pole in 1909.

Pemmican

Pemmican, a Cree word meaning "greased food," was Canada's first fast food. Explorers often carried this Native food when travelling because it cut down on the need for hunting. Pemmican was made by drying bear, buffalo or moose meat and pounding it into a powder, mixing it with berries and grease, then storing it in leather pouches.

Not only did just 1 kg (2¼ lb.) of pemmican equal the amount of protein in 4 kg (9 lb.) of fresh meat, it also wouldn't go bad. The Plains people produced and traded pemmican with the explorers and fur traders.

Rock Tripe

As well as eating animal skins and their own leather shoes when they were starving, explorers were often forced to eat a form of moss or lichen known as rock tripe. This plant that grows on rocks in the Arctic gave them enough protein to survive.

Rock tripe looks like dark lettuce and has a strong bitter taste. It must be boiled or its high acid content will upset starving stomachs. Hudson's Bay trader Samuel Hearne often ate rock tripe on his expedition to the Coppermine River in 1771.

"THEY PROCEED THROUGH THE MIDST OF THE SNOW WITH INCREDIBLE SWIFTNESS ... THEY PLACE BENEATH THEIR SOLES AND FASTEN TO THEIR FEET BROAD PIECES OF NETWORK."

— *Description of snowshoes from the Jesuit Relations*

EXPLORATION AND THE FUR TRADE

During the sixteenth and seventeenth centuries, hats made from beaver pelts became a fashion craze in Europe. The search for furs to meet this demand led to the further exploration of Canada.

But exploring this rugged land took time and cost money. So the fur traders turned to the kings of England and France for help. Permission from kings was given to companies of fur traders —

the Hudson's Bay Company and the North West Company — to expand the fur trade farther into Canada.

For 250 years, the fur trade employed thousands of people. The rivers the traders paddled and the trails they followed were like highways today. In fact, the Trans-Canada Highway follows the routes used by these early fur-trade explorers.

Freelance Traders

In the early days of trading, European ships sailed into the mouth of the St. Lawrence River and Native people paddled out to trade their furs for goods such as axes and knives. As the demand for furs increased, independent traders called *coureurs de bois*, or "runners of the woods," started travelling inland.

Voyageurs brought furs to the North West Company trading post at Fort William on the shore of Lake Superior (where the city of Thunder Bay stands today).

Radisson and Des Groseilliers

In the summer of 1660, two coureurs de bois, Pierre-Esprit Radisson and his brother-in-law Médard Chouart Des Groseilliers, arrived in Montreal with 100 canoes packed with furs. Instead of praising them, the governor of New France confiscated most of their furs because they were trading without a licence.

The two traders were furious about this, so they turned to British merchants. Radisson and Des Groseilliers were sure that bringing ships into Hudson Bay and setting up trading posts there was a way to make money trading furs.

Rupert's Land

Radisson and Des Groseilliers left England together to search Hudson Bay for furs. But Radisson had to turn around when his ship, the *Eaglet*, was damaged. Des Groseilliers was successful and returned to England with his ship, the *Nonsuch*, full of furs. This convinced King Charles II to support this fur-trade route. In 1670 the king granted his cousin, Prince Rupert, the rights to all the land surrounding the rivers that emptied into Hudson Bay — half of Canada. Prince Rupert sponsored the new Hudson's Bay Company (HBC).

History Today

You can see an exact replica of Des Groseilliers's ship the *Nonsuch* at the Manitoba Museum of Man and Nature in Winnipeg. It was built using seventeenth-century tools and methods.

Fur Traders Wanted

In 1684, an advertisement by the HBC convinced the Scottish teenager Henry Kelsey to leave his family and home and become a fur trader. For the next forty years, he was a faithful employee of the HBC.

Because of his ability to learn Native languages and his interest in their way of life, Kelsey was sent out to encourage more Native people to bring their furs to HBC trading posts. He became the first European to spend a long period of time living with the Plains people on the prairies.

◆ PROFILE ◆

ÉTIENNE BRÛLÉ

Étienne Brûlé was Canada's first coureur de bois. He was only fourteen in 1606 when he sailed from France to Canada with Samuel de Champlain. At sixteen, Brûlé chose to live with the Huron and became a skilled paddler. He even learned how to shoot rapids in his canoe. He also became fluent in the Huron language.

Travelling by canoe with the Huron, Brûlé was the first European to reach the Great Lakes. Later, Champlain used Brûlé's skill as a guide and interpreter to travel with him up the Ottawa River and as far west as Georgian Bay, Ontario.

Champlain felt betrayed by Brûlé because he helped the English defeat the French at Quebec. Brûlé was killed by the Huron in 1633 as punishment for betraying Champlain and working for the English.

The North West Company

At first, independent French traders in Montreal were competing for furs with the British HBC. After the fall of New France in 1759 to England, these traders joined a more organized group, made up of Scottish immigrants, and in 1779 formed the North West Company (NWC).

The traders and *voyageurs* (boatmen) who worked for the NWC were called Nor'Westers. Their headquarters was in Montreal, but their trading posts, eventually 342 of them, were to spread 4300 km (2700 mi.) across eastern and western Canada.

Family of Explorers

Pierre La Vérendrye (above) was a Quebec farmer who, along with his four sons, became an explorer and fur trader searching for a "western sea" in 1728. He was convinced that Lake Winnipeg in Manitoba would lead to the Pacific Ocean. To finance his exploration, La Vérendrye opened trading forts along his routes.

Samuel Hearne

When he was still a child, Samuel Hearne sailed around the world as a cabin boy in the British Navy. By age twenty-four, he was a trader with the HBC. Hearne loved animals and kept many pets at the trading post at Fort Prince of Wales. His zoo (above) included bald eagles, beavers, foxes, horned owls, lemmings and mink.

To prepare for his search for copper and the Coppermine River (located in today's Northwest Territories), Hearne toughened himself up by walking 485 km (300 mi.) between two forts on Hudson Bay. He also camped out all winter and practised running on snowshoes.

With Chipewyan chief Matonabbee as his guide, Hearne reached the mouth of the

FRANCES ANN HOPKINS

Although Native women often travelled with their husbands in early Canada, European women rarely did. One exception was artist Frances Ann Hopkins. She travelled to trading posts with her husband, who worked for the HBC.

On her trips into the interior in 1861 and 1869, Hopkins painted many portraits of voyageurs and their canoes. Although she lived in Canada for only eight years, her paintings are still well known and are displayed in many art galleries.

Coppermine River in 1771. He was disappointed that instead of copper he found only "a jumble of rock and gravel." But Hearne was the first European to reach the Arctic Ocean by land.

Peter Pond

In 1778, American Peter Pond of the NWC became the first fur trader to travel into the Athabasca country (in today's northern Alberta). The quality and quantity of furs he brought back made him a partner in the company.

Pond drew a map of the Mackenzie Basin area based on Native people's reports and his own explorations. Despite Pond's success as a trader, he had to leave the company because of his involvement in the murder of two traders from the rival HBC.

Dangerous Popularity

It's estimated that at the start of the fur trade there were ten million beavers in Canada. At the peak of the trade, 100 000 pelts were being shipped to Europe. Luckily for the beaver, by the 1800s Europeans' taste in hats had changed from fur to silk, and the beaver was saved from extinction.

History Today

By the early 1800s, furs were becoming scarce and American fur traders were starting to move into Canadian territory. So, in 1821, the HBC and the NWC decided to join together under the name of the Hudson's Bay Company. That company is still in business today — but the fur-trade posts have changed to department stores and the company name is now the Bay.

WEST COAST EXPLORATION

The exploration of the west coast of Canada didn't begin seriously until the late eighteenth century. Russian, Spanish and British explorers were interested in claiming the Pacific coast of Canada and hoped to find a Northwest Passage. The wild coastline was a good place for trading posts but not for settlement.

The Europeans believed they could make huge profits by developing a fur trade with the Native people on the northwest coast. The first people to explore the northern part of the coast were Russian. Then the Spanish came up from their colony in Mexico. But it was the British whose detailed maps of the coastline gave them claim to the land.

Russia's Expedition

In 1725, while exploring the most northern areas of Russia, the Danish explorer Vitus Bering discovered the Bering Strait. This narrow stretch of water proved that Asia and North America were two separate continents.

In 1741, Bering sailed to Alaska and traded with the Native people there for sea otter pelts. Bering's ship was wrecked, and he and five of his men died of scurvy on what was later called Bering Island. But because of Bering's explorations, Russia claimed ownership of the Alaska coast.

Spain's Exploration

The first Spaniard to explore the north Pacific coast was Juan Pérez Hernández. In 1774 he sailed as far as the Queen Charlotte Islands, where he met with the Haida people. He also traded with the Nootka on what was later called Vancouver Island before sailing back to Mexico.

The next year Hernández returned, along with Juan Francisco de la Bodega y Quadra. Their job was to search out the Russian posts and officially take possession of the area for Spain. They were successful in taking over some Russian posts,

When Europeans explored Canada's west coast, they met many tribes of Native people.

and Bodega y Quadra made charts of the British Columbia coast.

Hernández's ship had to return home with wounded crew members after battling with Native people on the present-day Washington coast. But Bodega y Quadra continued sailing along the British Columbia and Alaska coasts, making charts (see page 40) and naming points of land.

DID YOU KNOW

The first Chinese to settle in Canada came with fur trader John Meares in 1788 to develop trade between Canton, China, and Meares's post at Nootka Sound.

Nootka Sound Dispute

Britain claimed the area of Nootka Sound on Vancouver Island's coast based on George Vancouver's exploration, but Spain also claimed the area. When John Meares, a British trader, set up a trading post there in 1788, the Spanish were ready to declare war on Britain.

The British government sent Vancouver to make peace with the Spaniard Bodega y Quadra, who was in charge of the Nootka Sound area. The two became friends and Bodega y Quadra let the British stay.

After negotiation between Vancouver and Bodega y Quadra, Britain and Spain finally agreed to share trading rights on Canada's Pacific Coast.

◆ PROFILE ◆

GEORGE VANCOUVER

Englishman George Vancouver was determined to captain his own ship after sailing up Canada's northwest coast with James Cook (page 42) in 1778. His goal was to make a detailed map of this coastline by following every inlet.

In 1791, Vancouver left England with 100 men on two ships. It took them a full year of sailing around the southern tip of South America before they reached their starting point for the map, just north of San Francisco Bay.

Vancouver was meticulous. At one point, he and his officers rowed 1540 km (960 mi.) into a fjord to plot the coastline. Three years after they left England, Vancouver's map was completed to as far as what is now the British Columbia/Alaska border.

Even though Vancouver's navigation charts helped establish Britain's claim to the northwest Pacific coast, he spent the last two years of his life trying to earn money. He wrote an account of his travels, *A Voyage of Discovery*, but died in 1798 at age forty, a month before his book was published.

History Today

In August 1991, a Soviet-Danish research team found and excavated Vitus Bering's grave. Until then, his appearance had been a mystery. Forensic physicians used Bering's skull as a guide and succeeded in recreating his face.

TECHNOLOGY OF EXPLORATION IV:
MAP-MAKING

Since prehistoric times, people have felt the need to draw maps of where they live. Maps began as rough drawings in sand or snow or on cave walls. As people became more skilled, maps were engraved on stone or wood and painted on animal skins.

Later, instruments such as the compass and sextant (see pages 14 and 15) were used to plot locations according to latitude and longitude. Some of the findings from these early maps are still used. Today's maps are generated by computers, and use satellite cameras to calculate exact locations.

Maps versus Charts

Maps describe location by giving information about direction and distance. Charts show data about sea coasts. To draw accurate maps and charts in the sixteenth century, explorers needed precise observations, a knowledge of geography and mathematics and the use of navigational tools such as the astrolabe and cross-staff (see pages 14 and 15).

Charts record the shape of coastlines and the depth of the water offshore so sailors know where hidden rocks and dangerous shoals are located. Early charts recorded the coastline by taking soundings — throwing a weighted line overboard and noting when it touched bottom. The depth was measured in fathoms; one fathom equals about 2 m (6 ft.). Now sailors use electronic equipment called sonar to avoid hitting submerged rocks or getting stuck in shallow water.

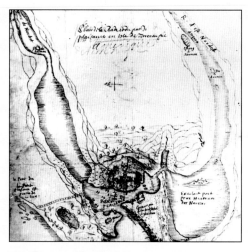

Harbour Charts

By 1502, Portuguese cartographers (map- and chart-makers) were creating enormous master charts containing all the latest knowledge of coastlines and oceans. Information from the voyages of the Portuguese Corte-Real brothers (see page 16) was used to create the first charts of Canada's east coast. These master charts were treated as state secrets, and few originals have survived.

As early as 1505, sailors needed charts with information about harbours' hidden rocks and shoals — called approach charts — in order to sail safely. Today sailors, as well as airline pilots, still use approach maps to warn about obstacles when entering a harbour or landing at an airport.

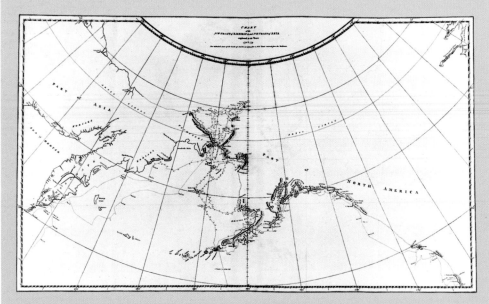

James Cook (see page 42) drew this map of the northwest coast of Canada in 1778.

Map Songs

Maps were expensive and often jealously guarded. Many skippers of fishing boats to the Grand Banks had to rely on rhyming poems that painted a picture of the coastline with words. These map songs were passed from generation to generation within a family, but very few were written down. One example that was written down in 1750 is "Wadham's Song," which maps 100 km (60 mi.) of Newfoundland's coast in eleven verses.

"If you draw near to Fogo Land
You'll have 15 fathoms in the
　　sounding sand;
From 15 to 18, never more
And that you'll have close to the shore"

— *Verse five of "Wadham's Song"*

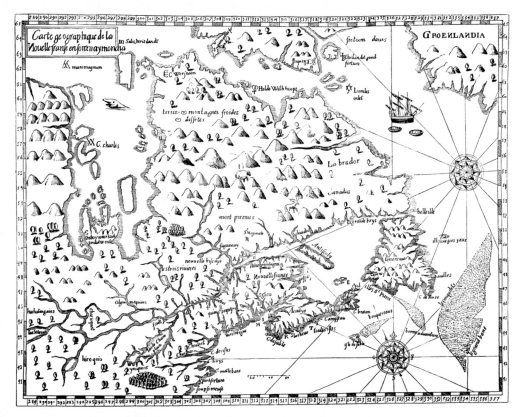

Carte geographique de la Nouvelle franse en son vray meridien

Early Maps of Canada

Most explorers kept careful records of land observations so that back in Europe they could have a map drawn by a professional map-maker. Some explorers, such as Samuel de Champlain, were also map-makers. Champlain's maps of eastern Canada from 1604 to 1635 (one is shown above) were a combination of his own latitude readings and the verbal descriptions and drawings given to him by Native people.

DID YOU KNOW

Many explorers paid the price, often their lives, for depending on maps with wrong information. Sometimes map-makers deliberately put mistakes on a map to stop competitors from finding a route the makers wanted to keep for themselves.

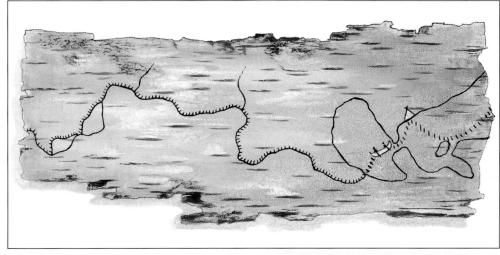

Time Maps

Inuit and Native people described their geography in terms of how long it took to get from one place to another. A map would be sketched with charcoal on birchbark or an animal skin and left in a tree, as a message for people travelling behind them. Because Native maps recorded locations based on time to reach them, not actual distance, Europeans found them confusing. The Hudson's Bay Company relied on the information that Natives gave them to draw maps of the areas around their trading posts.

Global Positioning Systems

Today, maps are created using readings sent back to Earth from satellites. Circling over Earth at a distance of about 20 000 km (12 400 mi.), twenty-four satellite cameras send signals that can pinpoint latitude and longitude readings anywhere on Earth.

CANADA'S MAP-MAKERS

I t's hard to imagine how to map a country as huge as Canada without the bird's-eye view of today's satellite cameras. But James Cook and David Thompson did it. Both these men, though born poor, educated themselves through reading and showing a great interest in everything they learned. Perhaps that's what made them such good map-makers.

Cook mapped the east and west coasts of Canada. Although better known for his explorations that led to the "discovery" of Australia and New Zealand, Cook was chosen to captain those voyages because of the excellent maps of Canada's east coast he made in the 1760s. About forty years later, Thompson mapped the interior of the Canadian west so thoroughly that every map of this vast area, until recently, was based on his work.

Cook sailing into Nookta Sound.

East Coast

As a captain in the British Navy, James Cook took part in many important events in Canadian history. In 1758, he helped enforce the British blockade of France's Fortress of Louisbourg in what's now Nova Scotia. Cook was General James Wolfe's navigator when they sailed down the St. Lawrence River in 1759 to defeat the French at the Battle of the Plains of Abraham in Quebec.

From 1762 to 1767, Cook mapped the intricate and treacherous coasts of Newfoundland and Labrador. He also trekked inland to survey Newfoundland's central highlands and lakes.

West Coast

The last of Cook's famous Pacific voyages was to search the west coast of Canada for the elusive Northwest Passage from the Atlantic Ocean. In 1778, he landed at Nootka Sound, then sailed north to the Beaufort Sea until pack ice made him turn back. All along Canada's west coast, he drew maps and searched for the passage. Cook planned to continue this work the following summer, but he was murdered in the Hawaiian Islands in 1779.

Thompson surveying the border between Canada and the United States.

Apprentice

When David Thompson (above) was growing up in a London orphanage, he was interested in two things: adventure stories and mathematics. In 1784, at age fouteen, Thompson was apprenticed to the Hudson's Bay Company and sailed to Canada to be a clerk.

At first, life in the cold trading post of Churchill Factory on the shores of Hudson Bay was not the exciting adventure Thompson was seeking. But soon he was included on expeditions inland and spent the winter learning the customs and language of the Peigan tribe. While recovering from a broken leg when he was eighteen, Thompson learned astronomy and map-making.

A New Job

Thompson left the Hudson's Bay Company in 1797 to become chief surveyor with its main competitor, the North West Company. The boundary lines between Canada and the United States had been decided, so the NWC needed someone to tell them in which country their trading posts were situated. When asked by the company to find a convenient route to the Pacific Ocean, Thompson explored and mapped the 1950 km (1200 mi.) of the Columbia River.

At Home in the Wilderness

Thompson's wife, Charlotte (who was Métis — a person of mixed European and Native descent), and their children often went with him on his survey trips. He had a good relationship with Native people, who respected his scientific knowledge and called him Koo Koo Sint — "Man Who Looks at Stars."

But Thompson could not find anyone to publish his journals or his five wall-sized maps. He died in poverty in 1857.

Milestone

When Cook set up his astronomy equipment at Nootka Sound on Vancouver Island's coast, he discovered he was 6400 km (4000 mi.) west of Newfoundland. This was the first measurement of Canada's massive width.

DID YOU KNOW

David Thompson was curious about everything. He made a point of tasting all species of moss, measuring antelopes' speed and taking the temperature of reindeer blood.

EXPLORING WILD RIVERS

Two explorers gave their names to the rushing rivers they explored. Alexander Mackenzie and Simon Fraser were teenagers when they became fur traders. Mackenzie joined the fur trade in 1779 and Fraser joined in 1792. Both men rose to the position of partner in the North West Company before it merged with the Hudson's Bay Company in 1821.

All fur-trade companies wanted to extend their system of trading posts as far west as the Pacific, and Mackenzie and Fraser each hoped to find a river that would provide a faster way of transporting furs to that coast.

The Mackenzie

In 1789, Alexander Mackenzie (left) followed a river from Great Slave Lake in today's Northwest Territories and was surprised to reach the Arctic Ocean. Though the expedition was an exciting exploration of Canada's longest river, Mackenzie was disappointed because it wasn't a route to the Pacific Ocean, so it was of no commercial use at the time. He called it the Disappointment River, but later it was named the Mackenzie River.

Pacific at Last

Four years later, Mackenzie was the first European to cross the Rocky Mountains by an overland route. Two Native guides took him along the "Grease Trail," named for the fish oil they obtained in trade with coastal tribes. When they reached the Pacific Ocean, Mackenzie took red dye, mixed it with bear grease and painted on a rock jutting into the Pacific Ocean "Alex Mackenzie from Canada by land 22d July 1793."

Mackenzie and his crew shooting rapids on the river that would later be named after him.

Power of the Pen

Like most explorers, Mackenzie kept a journal of his experiences in Canada. He described the vast country and the numerous Native tribes he met. When he returned to England in 1799, he published his journal with the title *Voyages from Montreal to the Frozen and Pacific Oceans*. It was a best-seller, and Mackenzie became one of the most famous explorers of his day.

Partner and Rival

Simon Fraser (above) became a partner in the North West Company when he was only twenty-five. Since Mackenzie's overland route was too long and dangerous to be a trade route, Fraser was asked by the NWC in 1808 to find a river route through the Rocky Mountains. He was very jealous of Mackenzie's fame and position in the company and was determined to outdo him.

A Dangerous Journey

Fraser chose to investigate an 840 km (520 mi.) river of turbulent waters and hair-raising cliffside portages. He hoped it would turn out to be the Columbia River, which had an established fur-trade fort at its mouth on the west coast. Fraser was too arrogant to listen to the warnings of a Native chief that "whirlpools will swallow up your canoes."

To encourage his men, Fraser gave his fragile birchbark canoes names such as *Perseverance* and *Determination*. But after facing many dangerous rapids, even Fraser admitted his trip was "a desperate undertaking." The men had to portage their loads along narrow paths while clinging to roots and branches. It was obvious that the river was too wild to be a transportation route for furs.

Fraser finally reached the Pacific Ocean, but when he used his sextant to establish his location, he found that this river was too far north to be the Columbia River. It was David Thompson, the map-maker and Simon Fraser's friend, who named the waterway the Fraser River.

History Today

You can follow in Mackenzie's footsteps because the last 350 km (220 mi.) of his expedition across Canada are now a hiking trail in British Columbia. The Alexander Mackenzie Heritage Trail stretches from the Fraser River at Quesnel to the coastal community of Bella Coola.

Fraser and his men crossing a dangerous cliff pass.

NORTHWEST PASSAGE REVIVAL

Hundreds of sailors and their ships lie buried beneath the frozen Arctic, lost in their quest for the Northwest Passage. Some historians even believe that John Cabot disappeared in 1498 on a search for this passage. James Cook attempted to find a passage from the west in 1778, but his ship was blocked by ice. For the next forty years, the British lost interest in the search.

But the end of a long war with France in 1815 found Britain with men and ships out of work. So the British Parliament offered a £20 000 reward (worth close to $2 million today) to the first ship to sail the Northwest Passage to the Pacific Ocean. The search was on again.

Wintering Over

Edward Parry (above) was the first Arctic explorer who deliberately spent a winter with his ships locked in the ice so he would have longer to explore. With his boats frozen at Melville Island in 1819, Parry grew medicinal herbs over the galley stovepipes and kept his men busy jogging. Even though he didn't find the passage, Parry was the first to return to England without losing one crew member.

Determined to Succeed

John Franklin first attempted to find a Northwest Passage in 1821 by charting the shores of the Arctic by land. This expedition was a disaster since ten of his men died from starvation. A second attempt (1825-1827) to chart the coast from the Coppermine River was successful thanks to the help of Native people.

In 1845, Franklin (right), his two ships, the *Erebus* and the *Terror,* and a crew of 140 men from the British Navy left to find the passage. The ships were equipped for a three-year trip with provisions that included fine china, a grand piano and a new invention — food in tins. No one ever heard from the expedition again.

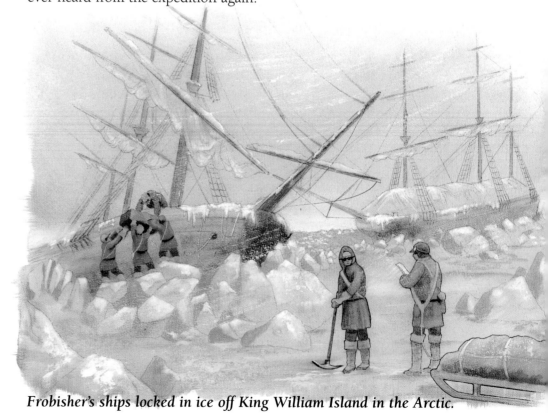

Frobisher's ships locked in ice off King William Island in the Arctic.

The Investigator

The Search
When no word of Franklin reached England by 1848, the greatest rescue operation in the history of exploration began. For the next sixteen years, more than thirty rescue parties searched for Franklin. Though he was never found, the searchers learned a lot more about the Arctic. Today scientists believe that many of Franklin's men may have died of lead poisoning from the solder used to seal their tin cans of food.

Success by Ice
While searching for Franklin in 1850, Robert McClure sailed the *Investigator* up the west coast of North America, through the Bering Strait and across the Beaufort Sea. His ship became trapped in ice, so

he went on by dogsled, becoming the first European to complete the Northwest Passage by sea and land.

Success by Water
In 1903, a young Norwegian named Roald Amundsen left Norway to study the magnetic forces of the North Pole. In 1906, his ship became the first to slip through the long, ice-filled waterway and reach the Pacific. This ended 400 years of searching for a Northwest Passage.

Milestone
In 1948, the Royal Canadian Mounted Police schooner *St. Roch*, powered by sail and engines, left Vancouver, sailed up the coast and navigated the Northwest Passage from west to east. The captain of the *St. Roch*, Henry Larsen, also brought it back across the passage in 1952. He was the first to sail the Northwest Passage in both directions.

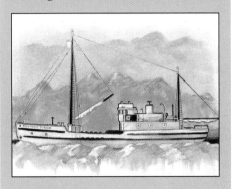

History Today
Now you can board the *St. Roch*, a National Historic Site, docked in Vancouver.

DID YOU KNOW

Even though several skeletons and articles belonging to the crew have been discovered, John Franklin's body has never been identified.

Amundsen and his ship the Gjoa.

RACE FOR THE NORTH POLE

By the end of the nineteenth century, most of Canada had been explored, except for the farthest point north. This area became the focus of an international race to reach the North Pole — the top of the world!

Reaching the pole meant braving frigid temperatures and fierce blizzard winds. The dangers faced by explorers travelling over the frozen Arctic Ocean included falling into deep crevasses, losing toes or fingers to frostbite or even freezing to death. During the short Arctic summer, the pack ice broke up in spots. This left wide, watery gaps called leads that explorers had to detour around.

Early Attempts

American Charles Hall mysteriously disappeared in 1871 trying to reach the North Pole, and another American expedition, led by Adolphus Greely, got only as far north as Ellesmere Island in 1885. In 1875, the British Navy's attempt to reach the pole, led by George Nares, also failed because he refused to use Inuit and Native devices such as igloos and snowshoes.

Bright Ideas

Scandinavian explorers had very imaginative ways of trying to reach the North Pole. In 1893, a Norwegian scientist, Fridtjof Nansen, built a strong ship, the *Fram* (above), to drift with the ice floes. However, it didn't pass as close to the North Pole as Nansen had hoped. Salomon Andree of Sweden tried to reach the pole in a hot-air balloon in 1897 but died in the attempt.

Arctic Dream

American naval officer and explorer Robert Peary (above left) read about the Arctic when he was six, and he described his dream of reaching the North Pole in his high-school graduation speech. By the time he was forty-two, he had made eight expeditions to the Arctic.

Peary and his friend Matthew Henson (above right) were accompanied by Inuit guides Egingwah, Ooqueah, Ootah and Seegloo on their trip in 1909. Peary and Henson persevered in their quest for the pole because they adopted traditional Inuit methods of frigid Arctic travel. They drove dogsleds over the ice, made igloos for their rest shelters and wore Inuit-style fur clothing to stay warm and dry.

Some of Peary and Henson's most difficult obstacles when driving dogsleds to the pole were pressure ridges — craggy hills of ice the size of four-storey buildings. These are created by colliding ice floes. Sometimes Peary's party had to drag their sleds over the tops of these hills rather than waste time on detours.

Peary kept checking the expedition's longitude and latitude. Finally, on April 6, 1909, the explorers believed they had reached the North Pole. Henson and the four Inuit men built an igloo and topped it with an American flag, while Peary photographed the historic moment.

True or False?

Whether Peary and Henson were the first to reach the North Pole or got there at all was argued for almost a century. Frederick Cook, who had been with them on a previous expedition, falsely claimed that he had reached the North Pole a year before.

This caused such a controversy that Peary and Henson's achievement was not fully accepted until a National Geographic Society investigation was done in 1990, long after both explorers had died. To this day, some experts still say there is no evidence to support Peary and Henson's claim.

Peary, Henson and crew dragging their sleds over a pressure ridge.

Milestone

In 1926, Norwegian Roald Amundsen flew a blimp (below left) over the North Pole. Later that year Americans Richard Byrd and Floyd Bennett flew over it in an airplane. The American nuclear submarine *Nautilus* (below right) made the first voyage under the pole in 1958.

"THE POLE AT LAST! MY DREAM AND GOAL FOR 20 YEARS."

— *Robert Peary's diary entry for April 6, 1909*

SCIENTIFIC EXPLORATION

As well as discovering new territories, explorers have always been interested in learning about the natural environment of these lands. With no cameras to record their explorations, many Europeans, such as Samuel de Champlain, Alexander Mackenzie and Jean de Brébeuf, sketched the animals, landscape and plants as a record of their voyages.

Later, the governments of Britain and Canada sponsored scientific expeditions, such as the one led by John Palliser from 1858 to 1863 to discover new plants, animals and resources such as coal, oil and precious metals.

Today, the Canadian government continues to sponsor scientific exploration through the Geological Survey of Canada and the Canadian Space Agency. Underwater exploration is carried out by the government's Oceanographic Fleet.

Canada's First Scientist

Michel Sarrazin came to Quebec in 1685 to be a doctor, but his first love was natural science. He explored the woods, fields and bogs of New France looking for unusual species of plants. He sent hundreds of sketches and specimens of animals, minerals, plants and rocks back to scientists in Paris, France.

DID YOU KNOW

Kicking Horse Pass in British Columbia was named after an incident involving James Hector, a member of John Palliser's expedition through the Rockies in 1858. Hector was kicked unconscious by a horse and almost buried alive by his men, who thought he was dead.

Canada's First Geologist

Canada's highest mountain is named in honour of William Logan, the first director of the Geological Survey of Canada. In order to complete his geological surveys, Logan often spent months in the wilds of present-day Ontario and Quebec, living in a tent. Logan's outstanding collection of Canadian minerals, including silver, copper and nickel, and his superb geological map of Canada were exhibited in London and Paris in the 1850s. This brought international attention to Canada's mineral wealth.

Minerals and Dinosaurs

Joseph Tyrrell (below) was a gold miner, historian and scientist who explored vast areas of northern and western Canada, filling in missing spots on the maps of the Northwest Territories. Tyrrell also edited the diaries of explorers Samuel Hearne and David Thompson.

In 1884, Tyrrell made a major dinosaur fossil discovery and also found Canada's largest coal deposit, both in Alberta. Later he made his fortune as a gold miner in the Klondike gold rush.

The Future

The frontiers for explorers in the twenty-first century are in outer space and under the oceans. The Canadian Space Agency was created in 1989 to train Canadian astronauts, develop satellites and run space science and technology programs.

Astronauts Roberta Bondar, Marc Garneau, Chris Hadfield, Steve MacLean, Julie Payette and Dave Williams have all flown on space-shuttle missions. These modern explorers have conducted research experiments in space, some involving the robotic Canadarm.

To help Canada's Oceanographic Fleet pursue underwater exploration, Phil Nuytten has developed submersible vehicles and diving suits that can withstand the pressure of deep water. This is allowing aquanauts to explore deeper reaches of the ocean floor.

Today, exploration in Canada continues in a different way. Modern explorers are scientists who want to understand Earth's ecosystems and try to preserve nature's wonders for future generations.

Canadarm aboard a space shuttle.

"IT WOULD HAVE BEEN TERRIBLE TO COME BACK TO EARTH AND NOT EXPLORE. WHEN I RETURNED TO EARTH, I SAW THINGS DIFFERENTLY."

— *Astronaut Roberta Bondar*

◆ PROFILE ◆

JULIE PAYETTE

Julie Payette grew up in Montreal, but she studied in schools and universities around the world, including Russia. In 1999 Payette rocketed into space on the American space shuttle *Discovery* and became the first Canadian to participate in a mission to deliver supplies to the International Space Station.

History Today

You can see some of the dinosaur bones found by Joseph Tyrrell at the Royal Tyrrell Museum of Palaeontology in Drumheller, Alberta.

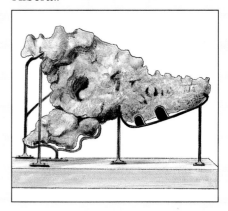

EXPLORERS' MAPS OF CANADA

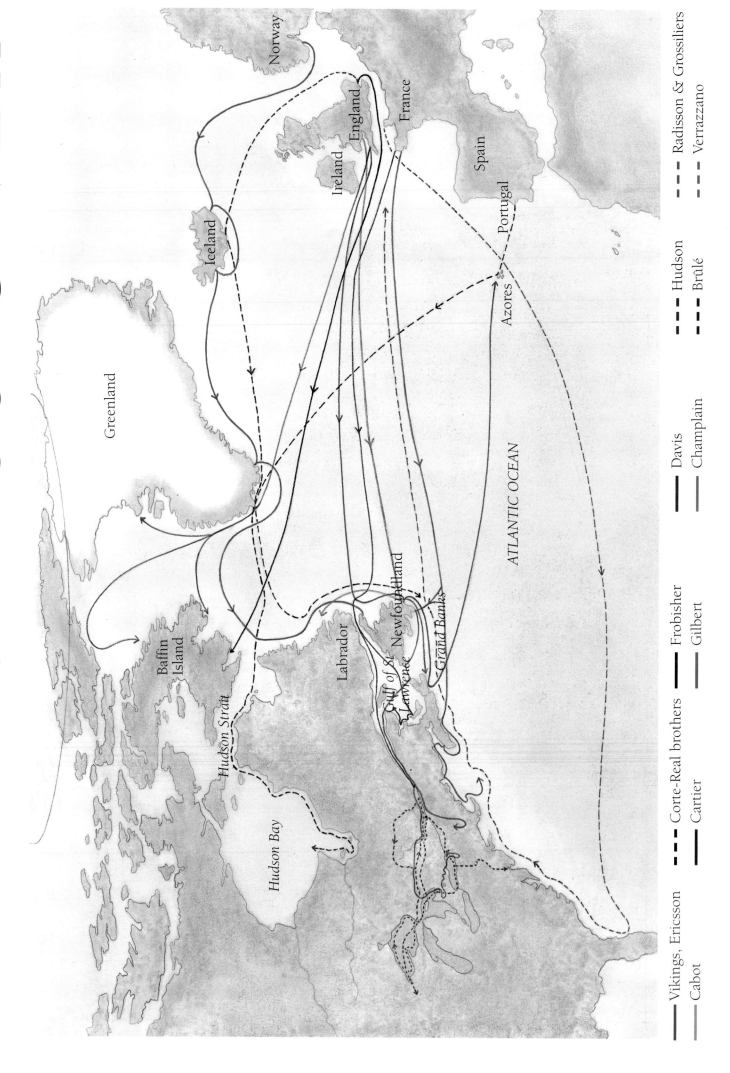

Legend:
— Vikings, Ericsson
— Cabot
--- Corte-Real brothers
— Frobisher
— Cartier
— Gilbert
— Davis
— Champlain
--- Radisson & Grossiliers
--- Hudson
--- Brûlé
--- Verrazzano

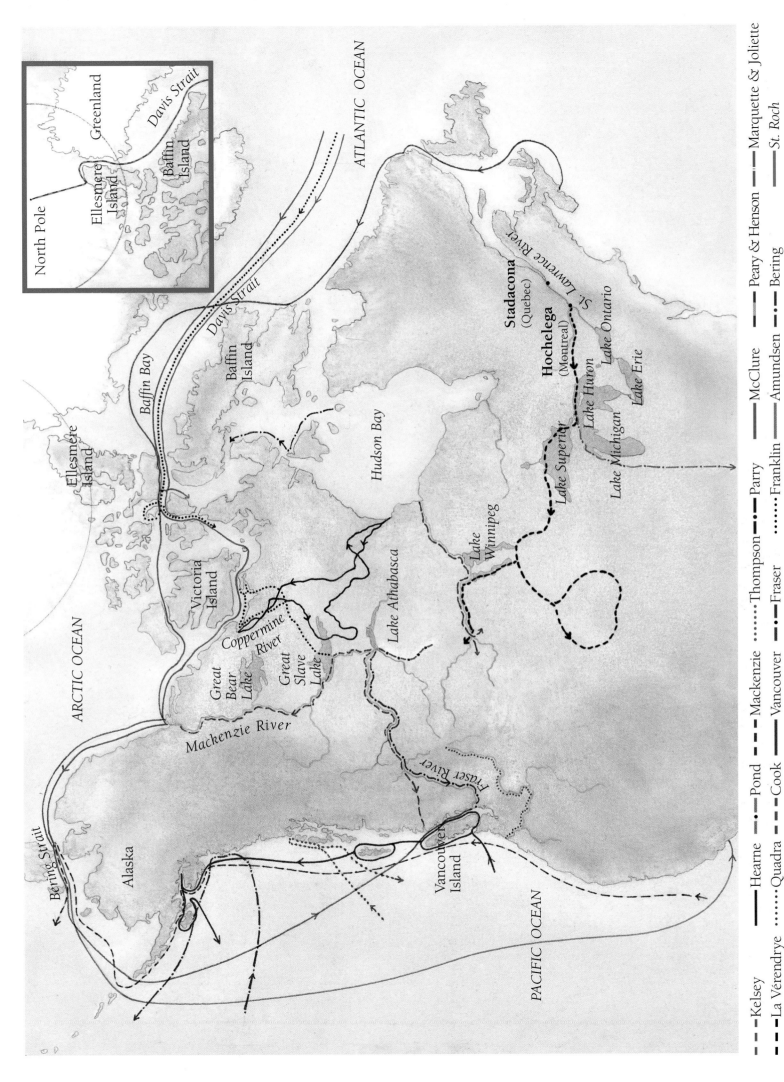

North Pole

Greenland
Ellesmere
Island
Baffin
Island
Davis Strait

ATLANTIC OCEAN

Davis Strait

Baffin Bay

Ellesmere
Island

Baffin
Island

Hudson Bay

Stadacona
(Quebec)

Hochelega
(Montreal)

St. Lawrence River

Lake Ontario

Lake Erie

Lake Huron

Lake Superior

Lake Michigan

Lake Winnipeg

ARCTIC OCEAN

Victoria
Island

Coppermine
River

Great
Bear
Lake

Great
Slave
Lake

Lake Athabasca

Mackenzie River

Fraser River

Bering Strait

Alaska

Vancouver
Island

PACIFIC OCEAN

Kelsey — Hearne —•• Pond — Mackenzie ••••• Thompson — McClure — Peary & Henson — Marquette & Joliette

La Vérendrye —•• Quadra — Cook — Vancouver ••••• Fraser —•— Franklin ••••• Parry — Amundsen — Bering — St. Roch

53

TIMELINE

Canadian Exploration		Canadian Events
	About 40 000 years ago	Ancestors of Canada's Native people may have migrated from Asia to North America
Native people explore North America	Thousands of years ago	
St. Brendan's legendary voyage to North America	500s	
Led by Leif Ericsson, Vikings arrive in Newfoundland and start colony	1000	
	1400s	European fisherman discover Grand Banks off Newfoundland
Portuguese sailors cross northern Atlantic Ocean to Greenland and Labrador	1440s	
Christopher Columbus discovers "New World" while searching for route to Asia	1492	
Treaty of Tordesillas divides world between Spain and Portugal	1494	
John Cabot's first voyage to "New Found Land" on Canada's east coast	1497	
Cabot and his ship disappear on his second voyage	1498	
Joao Fernandes as well as Gaspar and Miguel Corte-Real explore waters around Greenland and Newfoundland	1500	
Plains tribes become first to explore prairies on horseback	1500s	
Joao Alvarez Fagundes may have established colony on Cape Breton Island, Nova Scotia	1520	
Giovanni da Verranzzano explores east coast of North America	1523	
Jacques Cartier's first voyage to Gulf of St. Lawrence	1534	
Cartier's second voyage to Stadacona (Quebec City)	1535	
Cartier's third voyage to establish colony near Stadacona	1541	
	1550–60	Basque fishermen make Red Bay on Labrador's coast world's largest whaling port
Martin Frobisher makes three voyages in search of Northwest Passage (a route through North America to reach Asia)	1576–78	
Humphrey Gilbert claims Newfoundland for Britain	1583	
John Davis makes three voyages in search of Northwest Passage	1585–87	
Samuel de Champlain first comes to Canada on fur-trading expedition	1603	
	1604	Mathieu Da Costa becomes first known Black person in Canada
	1605	French build Port-Royal in Nova Scotia
Henry Hudson explores North America looking for Northwest Passage	1607–11	
Étienne Brûlé travels with Huron people and becomes first European to reach Great Lakes	1608	Samuel de Champlain founds Quebec
Hudson's crew mutinies and leaves Hudson, son and other crew members in Hudson Bay	1611	
Thomas Button searches for Hudson in Hudson Bay	1612	
Champlain explores from Quebec to Lake Huron by canoe	1614–16	
	1625	Jesuit priests arrive in Quebec to begin missionary work among Native people
Luke Fox and Thomas James explore Hudson Bay and James Bay	1631	
	1634–39	Huron people are almost wiped out by smallpox introduced by Europeans
	1642	Ville-Marie (Montreal) founded as missionary colony
Pierre-Esprit Radisson and Médard Chouart Des Groseilliers explore Canada's interior in search of beaver pelts	1660	
	1670	Hudson's Bay Company founded
Jacques Marquette and Louis Jolliet explore Mississippi River in search of Pacific Ocean	1673	
Scientist Michel Sarrazin explores New France	1685	
Henry Kelsey spends several years with Plains people exploring for Hudson's Bay Company	1690	
Pierre La Vérendrye and sons reach Lake Winnipeg	1728	
Vitus Bering explores northern Pacific coast	1741	

	1759	Britain defeats New France at Battle of the Plains of Abraham
James Cook explores and maps east coast of Canada	1762–67	
Samuel Hearne, with Native guide Matonabbee, explores Coppermine River. He becomes first European to reach Arctic Ocean by land.	1771	
Juan Pérez Hernández explores Pacific coast as far north as Queen Charlotte Islands	1774	
Hernández and Juan Francisco de la Bodega y Quadra map Pacific coast. Bodega y Quadra sails as far north as Alaska.	1775	
Peter Pond explores northern Alberta	1778	
Cook explores west coast of Canada		
	1779	North West Company formed
	1788	John Meares builds trading post on Vancouver Island, which almost leads to war between England and Spain
Alexander Mackenzie explores Mackenzie River	1789	
George Vancouver charts northwest coast	1791	Upper Canada and Lower Canada form
Mackenzie reaches Pacific Ocean by land. He becomes first European to cross Rocky Mountains by overland route.	1793	
David Thompson maps Columbia River	1797	
Simon Fraser explores Fraser River	1808	
	1812–14	War of 1812 between Britain (Canada) and United States
	1812	Red River settlement begins
	1818	Forty-ninth parallel accepted as border between Canada and United States
Edward Parry and entire crew successfully survive winter in Arctic	1819	
John Franklin makes first voyage in search of Northwest Passage	1821	North West Company merges with Hudson's Bay Company
Franklin's second voyage	1825–27	
	1841	Upper and Lower Canada join to form Province of Canada
	1843	Fort Victoria built by Britain to establish its claim to Vancouver Island
Franklin disappears on third exploration for Northwest Passage	1845	
Greatest rescue operation ever mounted fails to find Franklin in Arctic	1848–64	
Robert McClure is first to complete Northwest Passage by ship and dogsled	1850	
	1857	Ottawa becomes capital of Province of Canada
John Palliser leads scientific expedition to explore western Canada	1858–63	
	1858	Fraser River gold rush
	1861–69	Frances Ann Hopkins travels across Canada by canoe, painting voyageurs and fur traders
	1867	Dominion of Canada formed
	1869–70	Red River Rebellion
	1870	Hudson's Bay Company sells its territory to Canada
Joseph Tyrrell discovers dinosaur bones in Alberta	1884	
	1885	For his leadership in 1885 Resistance, Louis Riel hanged for treason
		Canadian Pacific Railway completed
Fridtjof Nansen on the *Fram* drifts past North Pole	1893	
	1897–99	Klondike gold rush
	1901	Gugliemo Marconi receives transatlantic radio message at St. John's, Newfoundland
Roald Amundsen first to sail through Northwest Passage	1906	
Robert Peary and Matthew Henson believe they reach North Pole	1909	
	1914–18	World War I
	1918	Women granted right to vote in federal elections
Amundsen flies blimp over North Pole	1926	
	1929–39	Great Depression
	1939–45	World War II
RCMP boat *St. Roch* becomes first to cross Northwest Passage in both directions	1952	
American submarine *Nautilus* is first to voyage under North Pole	1958	
	1960	Viking site at L'Anse aux Meadows, Newfoundland, excavated
	1965	Canada gets Maple Leaf flag
Marc Garneau becomes first Canadian astronaut in space	1984	
Julie Payette is first Canadian to board International Space Station	1989	Canadian Space Agency is created
	1999	Territory of Nunavut formed
	2001	Canadarm2 attached to International Space Station
Geological Survey of Canada explores Polar Continental Shelf to increase scientific knowledge and establish Canadian Arctic Sovereignty	2007	Northwest Passage ice free for first time in recorded history

INDEX